The Frog Prince

Retold by Daniel Jacobs

Illustrated by

Pamela Anzalotti

Rigby®

A Harcourt Achieve Imprint

www.Rigby.com
1-800-531-5015

My name is Cora, and I'd like to tell you about the day that changed my life forever. One afternoon I was rowing through muddy waters, which is not my favorite job. Why was I here in these muddy waters? My little sister Lisette wanted a ride. That's why!

My job was to keep Lisette out of trouble. Wherever she went, I went. While I paddled, Lisette played with her golden ball.

"Watch, Cora, I'll catch it with one hand!" she called.

"Careful, Lisette," I said, steering the shaky boat.

Suddenly, Lisette screamed like her hair was on fire!

I looked to see what she was screaming about.

"Hurry, Cora, my ball is sinking into the water!" Lisette sobbed.

Just then a frog leaped into Lisette's lap, holding Lisette's golden ball! "You may have this ball back if you take me home with you," the frog said.

Lisette tried to grab the ball away from the frog, but he hopped out of reach. "Let me eat from your plate and rest on your pillow. And, you must promise to kiss me goodnight." the frog said.

"OK, I promise!" Lisette agreed.

When we safely returned to shore, Lisette ran from the frog and into our house. The poor little frog hopped after her.

"Wait for me, Lisette," he called. "Remember your promise!"

But before the frog could reach our house, Lisette slammed the door.

I caught up to the frog and said, "I don't know why Lisette is so mean, but don't worry, Frog. I'll make sure you get dinner." I carefully put him in my pocket and went inside the house.

As soon as dinner was served, the frog jumped out of my pocket and onto the table. *Splat!* He landed right in the middle of Lisette's plate.

Papa looked upset. "Cora," he yelled, "get rid of that creature!"

Before I could grab the frog, he hopped onto Papa's shoulder and whispered into his ear.

"Did you make promises to this frog?" Papa asked Lisette.

"Yes, Papa," Lisette whispered.

"Then you must keep your promises," Papa told her.

So Lisette let the frog eat from her plate, but only after she covered her corn in hot sauce!

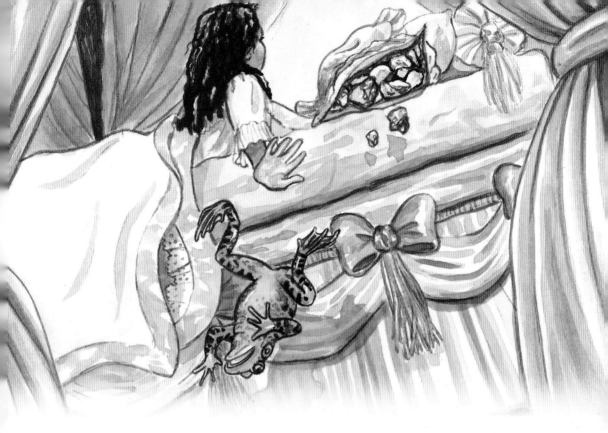

Lisette even let him rest on her pillow, but only after she had filled it with rocks! Still, the frog seemed happy and never said a word.

But I knew Lisette would never kiss the frog. When he hopped up onto her bed and asked for his kiss, Lisette rudely pushed him back onto the floor.

I didn't think that was very nice, so I picked up the frog and gently kissed his head. Then a surprising thing happened that changed my life forever.

Suddenly the frog changed into a handsome prince! "You freed me, Cora!" he shouted. "A mean witch cast a spell on me that turned me into a frog. I had to stay a frog until a human girl kissed me. Thank you for breaking the spell."

It turned out that Prince Eric was kind as well as handsome. He asked me to walk him home. His parents were so thankful that they invited me back for dinner the next day.

Kissing that frog changed my life forever, and I've never kissed another frog again. In the end, the prince and I were married and lived happily ever after.